If Your Nose Runs, And Your Feet Smell, Are You Upside Down?

Series:
Book One

If Your Nose Runs, And Your Feet Smell, Are You Upside Down?

(And Other Stupid Questions No One Really Needs to Know the Answers To)

Written by
Don Davis

If Your Nose Runs, And Your Feet Smell, Are You Upside Down? (And Other Stupid Questions No One Really Needs to Know the Answers To)

Alex Joseph Publishing
leadintoink@gmail.com
Burbank, California, U.S.A.

ISBN: 978-0-692-07856-3
ISBN 10: 0-692-07856-8

This book is dedicated to A) all the people that were there for me when it wasn't fashionable. To those who knew ME deep down. To those that influenced me. To those that stuck by me. To those that believed in me. To those that are no longer with me, but look down and smile upon me. To those who laughed WITH me. To those who helped shape my quirky sense of humor. To those who love me unconditionally. ------ I thank you from the bottom of my heart and know I could never repay your kindness and your love.

And B), to those who abused me. To those who doubted me. To those that laughed at me. To those that made fun of me. To those who went out of their way to make me stumble. To those who pulled the rug out from under me. To those who don't think you should be in this section because you are vile and in denial. ---- I forgive you.

If Your Nose Runs, And Your Feet Smell, Are
You Upside Down?

WHY?

Why do people never say, "it's only a game,"
when they're winning?

Why do people, when they hit or burn their
finger, automatically stick it in their mouth?

Why do people say they "slept like a baby,"
when babies wake up every few hours and
poop in their pants?

Why do superheroes wear their underwear
on the outside of their clothes?

If Your Nose Runs, And Your Feet Smell, Are You Upside Down?

Why do people say they only like the_____ colored M&M's? (pick your favorite color) Don't they all taste the same?

Why do shops have "Guide Dog Only" signs when dogs can't read, and their owners are blind?

Why is it called "tourist season" if we can't shoot them?

Why is there an expiration date on sour cream?

Why does caregiver and caretaker mean the same thing?

If Your Nose Runs, And Your Feet Smell, Are You Upside Down?

Why do they sterilize lethal injections?

Why is it that when we "skate on thin ice", we can "get in hot water"?

Why does quicksand work slowly?

Why is vanilla ice cream white, when vanilla extract is brown?

Why do we put suits in a garment bag and put garments in a suitcase?

Why do they call the little candy bars "fun sizes"? Wouldn't it be more fun to eat a big one?

If Your Nose Runs, And Your Feet Smell, Are You Upside Down?

Why are there no 'B' batteries?

Why does a round pizza come in a square box?

Why don't women put pictures of their missing husbands on beer cans?

Why do people say, "heads up," when you should duck?

Why do they lock the lid on a coffin?

If Your Nose Runs, And Your Feet Smell, Are You Upside Down?

Why do they call it the Department of Interior when they oversee everything outdoors?

Why do they call them "Free Gifts"? Aren't all gifts free?

Why do overalls have belt loops, since they are held up at the top by the straps?

Why are all the Harry Potter spells in Latin if they're English?

Why do we recite at a play, and play at a recital?

If Your Nose Runs, And Your Feet Smell, Are
You Upside Down?

Why are builders afraid to have a 13th floor,
but book publishers aren't afraid to have a
Chapter 11?

Why is it called a funny bone, when if you hit
it, it's not funny at all?

Why is the man who invests your money
called a "broker"?

Why are they called apartments when they
are all stuck together?

Why is it that people duck in the rain, do
they really think the rain won't hit them?

If Your Nose Runs, And Your Feet Smell, Are
You Upside Down?

Why didn't Noah swat those two mosquitoes?

Why do you need a driver's license to buy
liquor when you can't drink and drive?

Why does Sea World have a seafood
restaurant?

Why are elderly people often called "old
people" but children are never called "new
people"?

Why do they call someone "late" if they died
early?

If Your Nose Runs, And Your Feet Smell, Are You Upside Down?

Why do you give your two cents worth when it's only a penny for your thoughts?

Why do we have hot water heaters when hot water doesn't need to be heated?

Why do they make cars go so fast if it's illegal to go over the speed limit?

Why do they call it 'chili' if it's hot?

Why is it said that an alarm clock is going off when really, it's coming on?

If Your Nose Runs, And Your Feet Smell, Are
You Upside Down?

Why is the show called Unsolved Mysteries?
If they were solved, they wouldn't be
mysteries.

Why are things typed up, but written down?

Why do British people never sound British
when they sing?

Why is the name of the phobia for the fear of
long words
Hippopotomonstrosesquipedaliophobia?

Why do we scrub down and wash up?

If Your Nose Runs, And Your Feet Smell, Are
You Upside Down?

Why do people tell you when they are
speechless?

Why is it when two planes almost hit each
other, it is called a "near miss"?

Why do fat chance and slim chance mean the
same thing?

Why aren't there ever any guilty bystanders?

Why isn't the word 'gullible' in the dictionary?

If Your Nose Runs, And Your Feet Smell, Are You Upside Down?

Why does Donald Duck wear a towel when he comes out of the shower, when he doesn't usually wear any pants?

Why is "number" abbreviated as "no" when there is no "o" in number?

Why do we teach kids that violence is not the answer and then have them read about wars in school that solved problems?

Why do people say PIN number when that truly means Personal Identification Number Number?

If Your Nose Runs, And Your Feet Smell, Are You Upside Down?

Why is it that on the back of a medicine bottle it says "adult" is 12 and above, but the adult age in reality is 18?

Why do people say, "You've been working like a dog," when dogs just sit around all day?

Why are there pictures of the sun wearing sunglasses when the purpose of sunglasses is to protect your eyes from the sun?

Why is it that when you transport something by car it is called shipment, but when you transport something by ship it's called cargo?

If Your Nose Runs, And Your Feet Smell, Are
You Upside Down?

Why do we put suits in a garment bag and
put garments in a suitcase?

Why do they put memory foam in a casket?
(this is absolutely true.)

If Your Nose Runs, And Your Feet Smell, Are
You Upside Down?

IF?

If you tried to fail, but succeeded, did you
fail, or did you succeed?

If one synchronized swimmer drowns, do the
rest drown too?

If a parsley farmer was sued, can the court
garnish his wages?

If a deaf child signs swear words, does his
mother wash his hands with soap?

If Your Nose Runs, And Your Feet Smell, Are You Upside Down?

If money doesn't grow on trees, then why do banks have branches?

If pro and con are opposites, wouldn't the opposite of progress be congress?

If glassblowers inhale, do they get stomach panes?

If ghosts can walk through walls and glide down stairs, why don't they fall through the floor?

If a mime is arrested, do they tell him he has a right to talk?

If Your Nose Runs, And Your Feet Smell, Are
You Upside Down?

If a bunch of cats jump on top of each other,
is it still called a dog pile?

If God sneezes, what would you say to Him?

If a jogger runs at the speed of sound, can
he still hear his iPod?

If the Cincinnati Reds were the first major
league baseball team, who did they play?

If one man says, "it was an uphill battle,"
and another says, "it went downhill from
there," how could they both be having
troubles?

If Your Nose Runs, And Your Feet Smell, Are You Upside Down?

If a bee has allergies, would it get hives?

If a deaf person has to go to court, is it still called a hearing?

If you steal a clean slate, does it go on your record?

If a criminal turns himself in, does he get the reward money?

If there's a speed of sound and a speed of light, is there a speed of smell?

If Your Nose Runs, And Your Feet Smell, Are You Upside Down?

If Wile E. Coyote had enough money to buy all that ACME stuff, why didn't he just buy dinner?

If you were driving at the speed of light and turned on your headlights, what would happen?

If parents say, "Never take candy from strangers," then why do we celebrate Halloween?

If sheep have wool, and it rains, why don't they shrink? And for that matter, if your t-shirt is 100 percent cotton and you wash and dry it, won't it shrink? So why don't cotton plants shrink after it rains and then the sun comes out?

If Your Nose Runs, And Your Feet Smell, Are You Upside Down?

If London Bridge is standing why is there a song about it falling down?

If a guy that was about to die in the electric chair had a heart attack, should they revive him, so they can do it themselves?

If you dug a hole through the center of the earth, and jumped in, would you stay at the center because of gravity?

If a grenade was thrown into a kitchen in France, would the result be called Linoleum Blown-a-part?
If the Dahlia Llama walked into a Pizza Place, would he tell the guy to "Make me one with everything"?

If Your Nose Runs, And Your Feet Smell, Are You Upside Down?

If your nose runs and your feet smell, are you upside down?

If you think nobody cares, try missing a couple of house payments.

If I had a dollar for every time I got distracted...Oh wow, its 3:00 am.

If you say the word "gullible" extremely slow it sounds like the word "oranges."

If a cow laughs, does milk come out of her nose?

If Your Nose Runs, And Your Feet Smell, Are You Upside Down?

If flying is so safe, why do they call the airport, the terminal?

If you throw a cat out of the house, does it become kitty litter?

If they always say Take 2 aspirins, why not increase the size of ONE?

If you choke a Smurf, what color does it turn?

If the Convenient store is open 24 hours a day, 365 days a year, why does it have locks on the door?

If Your Nose Runs, And Your Feet Smell, Are You Upside Down?

If a firefighter fights fire and a crime fighter fights crime, what does a freedom fighter fight?

If they squeeze olives to get olive oil, do they squeeze babies to get baby oil?

If you only have one eye...are you blinking or winking?

If marbles are not made of marble, why are they called marbles?
If you have a cold hot pocket, is it just a pocket?

If Your Nose Runs, And Your Feet Smell, Are You Upside Down?

If an anarchist group attained political power, would they have to dissolve their own government just out of principle?

If you decide that you're indecisive, which one are you?

If Americans throw rice at weddings, do the Asians throw hamburgers?

If practice makes perfect, and nobody's perfect, then why do we practice?

If there's an exception to every rule, is there an exception to that rule?

If Your Nose Runs, And Your Feet Smell, Are You Upside Down?

If electricity comes from electrons, does morality come from morons?

If the weatherman says, "Today there is a 50% chance of rain" does that mean he really has no idea if it's going to rain or not, and he is just playing it safe?

If a person suffered from amnesia and then was cured would they remember that they forgot?

If you drive by those road signs that say, "Do Not Pass" are you breaking the law?

If Your Nose Runs, And Your Feet Smell, Are
You Upside Down?

If a General is a higher-ranking officer than a
Major, then why is a major illness worse than
a general illness.

If something "goes without saying," why do
people still say it?

If you jog backwards, will you gain weight?

If you can't drink and drive, why do bars
have parking lots?

If you ate pasta and antipasta, would you
still be hungry?

If you can't reach it, do you really need it?

If Your Nose Runs, And Your Feet Smell, Are You Upside Down?

If Geronimo jumped out of a plane, what would he yell?

If you put a sheet over your head for Halloween, are you a ghost or a mattress?

If water spins clockwise when it drains in the northern hemisphere, and water spins counterclockwise when it drains in the southern hemisphere...which way does it spin at the equator?
If a boy is named after his dad, he is called 'Junior,' but what do you call a girl that is named after her mother?

If Your Nose Runs, And Your Feet Smell, Are You Upside Down?

If there is a rule that states "i" before "e" except after "c", wouldn't "science" be spelled wrong?

If prunes are dehydrated plums, where does prune juice come from?

If quitters never win, why do they tell us to quit while we're ahead?

If you had a three-story house and were on the second floor, isn't it possible that you can be upstairs and downstairs at the same time?

If people with one arm go to get their nails done, do they pay half price?

If Your Nose Runs, And Your Feet Smell, Are You Upside Down?

If you put a chameleon in a room full of mirrors, what color would it turn?

If we aren't supposed to eat at night, why do they put lights in refrigerators?

If I got 50 cents for every math test I failed in school, I'd have $9.14

If Your Nose Runs, And Your Feet Smell, Are You Upside Down?

DO, DOES and DOESNT

Do pigs pull their ham strings?

Don't you hate it when someone answers their own questions? I know I do.

Do the English people eat English muffins, or are they just called muffins?

Do coffins have lifetime guarantees?

Do the security guards at airports have to go through airport security when they get to work?

If Your Nose Runs, And Your Feet Smell, Are You Upside Down?

Do atheists that have insurance get paid for an act of God?

Do dentists go to other dentists or do they just do it themselves?

Do prison buses have emergency exits?

Do astronauts change their clocks when they move over different time zones in space?

Do we sweat when we swim?

Do illiterate people get the full effect of Alphabet Soup?

If Your Nose Runs, And Your Feet Smell, Are
You Upside Down?

Does a group of cannibals that eat a
missionary get a taste of religion?

Does a group of cannibals that eat a man
dressed as a clown tell the cook that their
meal tasted funny?

Does a backward poet write inverse?

Doesn't "expecting the unexpected" make
the unexpected, expected?

Do one legged ducks swim in circles?

Do Roman paramedics refer to IV's as 4's?

If Your Nose Runs, And Your Feet Smell, Are You Upside Down?

Do pilots take crash-courses?

Do fish get thirsty?

Do sheep get static cling when they rub against one another?

Does it really count in court when an atheist is sworn in under oath using a Bible?

If Your Nose Runs, And Your Feet Smell, Are You Upside Down?

FROM THE NEWSROOM...Wait, Whaaaa?

*THIS JUST IN...*Vandals knock hole in nudist camp wall. Authorities are looking into it.

*THIS JUST IN...*Something went wrong in jet crash experts say.

*THIS JUST IN...*Man kills self before shooting wife and neighbor.

*THIS JUST IN...*Police begin campaign to run down Jaywalkers.

If Your Nose Runs, And Your Feet Smell, Are You Upside Down?

THIS JUST IN... Panda mating fails: Veterinarian takes over.

THIS JUST IN... Miners refuse to work after death.

THIS JUST IN... Juvenile Court to Try shooting Defendant

THIS JUST IN... War dims hope for peace.

THIS JUST IN... If strike isn't settled quickly, it may last awhile.

If Your Nose Runs, And Your Feet Smell, Are
You Upside Down?

THIS JUST IN...Arctic air linked to cold
temperatures.

THIS JUST IN...Local couple slain:
Authorities suspect homicide.

THIS JUST IN...Red Tape holds up new
bridge.

THIS JUST IN...Obesity study looks for
larger test group.

THIS JUST IN...Kids make nutritious snacks
for neighbors.

If Your Nose Runs, And Your Feet Smell, Are You Upside Down?

THIS JUST IN... Local High School dropouts cut in half

THIS JUST IN... Thief steals calendar. Gets twelve months.

THIS JUST IN... Man who fell in an upholstery machine was fully recovered.

THIS JUST IN... Police called to day care at nap time. Three-year-old resisted a rest.

THIS JUST IN... Typhoon slams cemetery. Hundreds Dead

If Your Nose Runs, And Your Feet Smell, Are You Upside Down?

THIS JUST IN... Police are looking for a mugger who threatens his victims with a lit match...
They need to catch him before he strikes again.

THIS JUST IN... Two men break into a drugstore and stole all the Viagra. The police say the public should be on the lookout for two hardened criminals.

If Your Nose Runs, And Your Feet Smell, Are You Upside Down?

WHEN AND WHERE?

When does it stop being partly cloudy and start being partly sunny?

When the French swear do they say pardon my English?

Where do forest rangers go to "get away from it all"?

When dog food is new and improved tasting, who tests it?

If Your Nose Runs, And Your Feet Smell, Are You Upside Down?

Where in the nursery rhyme does it say humpty dumpty is an egg?

Where did Webster look up the definitions when he wrote the dictionary?

When night falls who picks it up?

When day breaks who fixes it?

When sign makers go on strike, is anything written on their signs?

When crazy people walk through the forest, do they take the psycho path?

If Your Nose Runs, And Your Feet Smell, Are
You Upside Down?

When two men get married to each other, do
they both go to the same bachelor party?

When lightning strikes the ocean, why don't
all the fish die?

When she saw her first strands of gray hair,
she thought she'd dye.

When a clock is hungry can it go back four
seconds?

When you've seen one shopping center
you've seen a mall.

If Your Nose Runs, And Your Feet Smell, Are You Upside Down?

When the smog lifts in Los Angeles, U.C.L.A.

When fish are in schools they sometimes take debate.

If Your Nose Runs, And Your Feet Smell, Are You Upside Down?

CINNAMON PUNS

There was the person who sent ten puns to friends, with the hope that at least one of the puns would make them laugh. No pun in ten did.

Two Eskimos sitting in a kayak were chilly, so they lit a fire in the craft. Unsurprisingly it sank. This action *proves* that you can't have your kayak and heat it too.

Two hydrogen atoms meet. One says, 'I've lost my electron.' The other says 'Are you sure?' The first replies, 'Yes, I'm positive.'

If Your Nose Runs, And Your Feet Smell, Are You Upside Down?

Two fish swim into a concrete wall. One turns to the other and says 'Dam!'

The roundest knight at King Arthur's round table was Sir Cumference. He acquired his size from too much pi.

I thought I saw an eye doctor on an Alaskan island, but it turned out to be an optical Aleutian.

She was only a whiskey maker, but he loved her still.

If Your Nose Runs, And Your Feet Smell, Are You Upside Down?

A rubber band pistol was confiscated from algebra class, because it was a weapon of math disruption.

A dog gave birth to puppies near the road and was cited for littering.

Two silk worms had a race. They ended up in a tie.

Time flies like an arrow. Fruit flies like a banana.

Two hats were hanging on a hat rack in the hallway. One hat said to the other: 'You stay here; I'll go on a head.'

If Your Nose Runs, And Your Feet Smell, Are
You Upside Down?

A vulture boards an airplane, carrying two
dead raccoons. The stewardess looks at him
and says, 'I'm sorry, sir, only one carrion
allowed per passenger.'

If Your Nose Runs, And Your Feet Smell, Are You Upside Down?

HOW?

How can something be "new" and "improved" if it's new? What were they improving on if it was new?

How far east can you go before you're heading west?

How fast do hotcakes sell?

How do you write zero in Roman numerals?

How many countries have July 4th? All of them. They don't skip from the 3rd to the 5th of July.

If Your Nose Runs, And Your Feet Smell, Are You Upside Down?

How do you get off a nonstop flight? How can you chop down a tree and then chop it up?

How can there be "self-help GROUPS"?

How come you pay extra to get something put on your hamburger, but they don't take off the price, if you get something taken off?

How can people be intolerant to intolerance?

How important does a person have to be before they are considered assassinated, instead of just murdered?
How much deeper would the ocean be without sponges?

If Your Nose Runs, And Your Feet Smell, Are You Upside Down?

How can someone be dirt poor, and another person be filthy rich?

How does the guy, who drives the snowplow, get to work?

How many of you believe in psycho-kinesis? Raise my hand.

If Your Nose Runs, And Your Feet Smell, Are
You Upside Down?

_IS_

Is there another word for "synonym"?

Is there a difference between normal ketchup
and fancy ketchup?

Is it even possible to have a civil war?

Is a pessimist's blood type B-negative?

Is there a time limit on fortune cookie
predictions?

If Your Nose Runs, And Your Feet Smell, Are You Upside Down?

Is it good if a vacuum really sucks?

Is it OK to use the AM radio in the afternoon?

Is a hot car, cool or is a cool car, hot?

Is drilling for oil, boring?

Isn't it funny how the word 'politics' is made up of the words 'poli' meaning 'many' in Latin, and 'tics' as in 'bloodsucking creatures'?

Is a Local Area Network in Australia called The LAN down under

If Your Nose Runs, And Your Feet Smell, Are
You Upside Down?

WHAT?

What if there were no hypothetical
questions?

What was the best thing since sliced bread
before sliced bread?

What is a picture of a thousand words worth?

What was Captain Hook's name before he
got the hook?

What do they call male meter maids?
What do you call a male ladybug?

If Your Nose Runs, And Your Feet Smell, Are
You Upside Down?

What do chickens think we taste like?

What do people in China call their good
plates?

What's the opposite of opposite?

What is the speed of dark?

If Your Nose Runs, And Your Feet Smell, Are
You Upside Down?

HMMMM

Whose cruel idea was it for the word "lisp" to
have "s" in it?

Can vegetarians eat animal crackers?

Would a fly without wings be called a walk?

Can a short person "talk down" to a taller
person?

Can you buy an entire chess set in a pawn
shop?

If Your Nose Runs, And Your Feet Smell, Are You Upside Down?

Did you hear about the fellow whose whole left side was cut off? He's all right now.

Have you noticed since everyone has a cell phone with built in cameras these days, no one talks about seeing UFOs like they used to?

I was polite today. I said "PLEASE" Well actually, I said "Bitch, PLEASE?!?!"

If Snapchat has taught me anything, it's that a lot of women look much better as farm animals.

If Your Nose Runs, And Your Feet Smell, Are You Upside Down?

My first wife left me because I kept pretending I was a Transformer. I begged her to stay by saying, "I can change."

I asked God for a bike, but I know God doesn't work that way, so I stole a bike and asked for forgiveness.

Shouldn't there be a sign on the lawn at the drug rehabilitation clinic that says, 'Keep off the Grass.'?

Did you hear about the Buddhist who refused Novocain during a root canal? His goal: transcend dental medication.

If Your Nose Runs, And Your Feet Smell, Are You Upside Down?

Can a cemetery raise its prices and blame it on the cost of living?

2 cannibals were eating a male missionary. One started at the feet and the other one started at the head.
The one at the head said to the other, "How are you doing?" The other one replied, "I'm having a ball!" to which the first one said, "Hey, slow down. You're eating too fast."

With her marriage, she got a new name and a dress.

Show me a piano falling down a mineshaft and I'll show you A-flat miner.

If Your Nose Runs, And Your Feet Smell, Are You Upside Down?

You are stuck with your debt if you can't budge it.

Whenever an adult is kidnapped, why isn't it called adult napped?

Which side is the other side of the street?

I couldn't work out how to fasten my seatbelt. Then it clicked.

Before they invented drawing boards, what did they go back to?

If Your Nose Runs, And Your Feet Smell, Are
You Upside Down?

Have you ever noticed that if you rearranged
the letters in mother in law, they'd come out
as Woman Hitler?

Support bacteria. They're the only culture
most people have.

In a democracy it's your Vote that counts. In
feudalism it's your Count that votes.

I used to eat a lot of natural foods until I
learned that most people die of natural
causes.

The easiest way to find something lost
around the house is to buy a replacement.

If Your Nose Runs, And Your Feet Smell, Are You Upside Down?

The dead batteries were given out free of charge.

A dentist and a manicurist married. They fought tooth and nail.

Its ok if you disagree with me, I can't force you to be right.

The professor discovered that her theory of earthquakes was on shaky ground.

The statistics on sanity say that one out of every four persons is suffering from some sort of mental illness. Think of your three best friends. If they're OK, then is it you?

If Your Nose Runs, And Your Feet Smell, Are You Upside Down?

I saw that. -Karma

If you fall, I will always be there. -Floor

Why is there so much month left at the end of the money?

Remember to set your scales back 10 lbs. this week.

PMS jokes aren't funny. Period.

What is the difference between snowmen and snowwomen?
Snowballs.

If Your Nose Runs, And Your Feet Smell, Are
You Upside Down?

One snowman asks another, "Do you smell
carrots?"

Speaking of snowmen, why did the snowman
pull down his pants?
He heard the snow blower was coming.

A cat and a frog were talking, when the cat
said, "I have more lives than you." The frog
said, "Oh yeah? You only have 9 lives, but I
croak hundreds of times a night."

Instead of "the John," I call my toilet "the
Jim." That way it sounds better when I say I
go to the Jim, first thing every morning.

If Your Nose Runs, And Your Feet Smell, Are You Upside Down?

I hate being Bipolar, it's great.

Health nuts are going to feel stupid someday, lying in hospitals, dying of nothing.

I've been diagnosed with a chronic fear of giants. I think the clinical term for it is Fee-fi-phobia.

Sticks and stones may break my bones, but words will never hurt me. Unless you get hit in the head with a dictionary.

All of us could take a lesson from the weather. It pays no attention to criticism.

If Your Nose Runs, And Your Feet Smell, Are You Upside Down?

In the 60s, people took acid to make the world weird. Now the world is weird, and people take Prozac to make it normal

I went to a bookstore and asked the salesclerk, "Where's the self-help section?" She said if she told me, it would defeat the purpose.

He had a photographic memory, which was never developed.

Christmas - What other time of the year do you sit in front of a dead tree and eat candy out of your socks?

If Your Nose Runs, And Your Feet Smell, Are You Upside Down?

If I build a stage made from old library books and have a production of Hamlet performed on it, would that be considered a Play on words?

My neighbor just found out she has diabetes, and now she won't make me cupcakes anymore. Why do bad things always happen to me?

My neighbor used to work as an electrician until he was discharged.

Teacher: "Where was the United States Constitution signed?"
Student: "At the bottom of the page!"

If Your Nose Runs, And Your Feet Smell, Are You Upside Down?

On the first day of school, the teacher asked a student, "What are your parents' names?" The student replied, "My father's name is Laughing and my mother's name is Smiling." The teacher said, "Are you kidding?" The student said, "No, Kidding is my brother. I am Joking."

What happens once in a minute and twice in a moment but never in a decade?
The letter "m."

My friend was selling sausages over the internet and he sent me a link.

You'd think a snail would be faster without its shell, but, it's more sluggish.

If Your Nose Runs, And Your Feet Smell, Are You Upside Down?

I went to the job center yesterday and asked if they had any jobs moving furniture, but they told me to "Take a seat."

My brother is so stupid, he failed his urine, blood and stress tests.

Wife: "What does IDK stand for?"
Husband: "I don't know."
Wife: "OMG, nobody does!"

When I was young, I was thrown out of the pool at the YMCA for peeing in the pool. This upset my Dad and he went right down there to find out what happened. The lifeguard told him I peed in the pool. But my Dad told him "C'mon, everyone pees in the pool!" The lifeguard said to my dad, "Yeah, but not from the diving board."

If Your Nose Runs, And Your Feet Smell, Are
You Upside Down?

I figured I would buy Velcro for my shoes
instead of laces. Why knot?

6:30 is the best time on a clock. Hands
down.

What gets wetter and wetter, the more it
dries? A towel.

I love the way the earth rotates. It really
makes my day.

When I was in High School, we went to a
Soda manufacturing factory. The next day
we all had a pop quiz.

If Your Nose Runs, And Your Feet Smell, Are You Upside Down?

A little kid was out trick-or-treating on Halloween dressed as a pirate. He rang a house's doorbell and the door was opened by a lady. "Oh, how cute! A little pirate! And where are your buccaneers?" she asked. The boy replied, "Under my buckin' hat."

I didn't like my beard at first. Then it grew on me.

If I had to describe myself in only 3 words, I guess it would be "Not very good in math."

I am addicted to drinking brake fluid, but don't worry, I can stop any time.

If Your Nose Runs, And Your Feet Smell, Are You Upside Down?

I was addicted to the Hokey Pokey, but I turned myself around.

I tried to drown all of my troubles. But she wouldn't go swimming.

I had a German shepherd that loved to drink unleaded fuel. One day she drank a whole bunch of it and started to run around the yard like crazy. My neighbor watched her run and run until the shepherd just stopped and laid down. My neighbor asked me if I thought the dog was OK. I told him she was fine, she just ran out of gas.

I think I bought some shoes from a drug dealer. I don't know what he laced them with, but I've been tripping all day.

If Your Nose Runs, And Your Feet Smell, Are You Upside Down?

I refused to believe my father was stealing from his job as a road worker. But when I got home all the signs were there.

I just bought a vintage Rolls Royce, but the I can't afford a driver. So, I spent all that money, and I've got nothing to chauffeur it.

I'm a schizophrenic and so am I.

OMG Piglet always stinks so bad. Maybe because he always plays with Pooh

I bought a new yard trimmer today. It's cutting hedge technology.

If Your Nose Runs, And Your Feet Smell, Are You Upside Down?

Why do penguins eat fish? Because donuts get soggy before they can catch them.

When you are on the computer, and you see a post about how to prevent coughs and sneezes don't click on it!! It's a virus.

How many fishermen does it take to change a light bulb? One, but you should have seen the bulb, it must have been THIS big.

What did the pirate say on his 80th birthday? Aye Matey. (say it fast)

What us a pirate's favorite letter? Most people say Rrrrrrrrr but no, it's the C.

If Your Nose Runs, And Your Feet Smell, Are
You Upside Down?

If the RED house is on the RED side and the
BLUE house is on the BLUE side, where is the
WHITE house? Washington D.C.

What do you call a boomerang that doesn't
work? A stick.

Cinderella was cut from the team today
because she kept running away from the
ball.

Pancakes and baseball, both need the same
thing. A good batter.

If Your Nose Runs, And Your Feet Smell, Are You Upside Down?

Two midgets go into a bar, where they pick up two ladies. They both take them to their separate hotel rooms. The first midget, forgot his Viagra and couldn't get a "woody." He was so embarrassed that the lady left. To make matters worse, he hears his buddy yelling "ONE, TWO, THREE...UUH!" from the next room, continuously, all-night long. In the morning, the second midget asks the first, "How did it go?" The first whispered back, "It was so embarrassing. No matter what I did, I couldn't get a "woody". The second midget shook his head. "You think that's embarrassing?" he asked. "I couldn't even get on the friggin' bed."

A duck walks into a bar and says to the bartender:" Got any grapes?" The bartender looks at the duck kind of weird and says "No,

If Your Nose Runs, And Your Feet Smell, Are You Upside Down?

I don't have any grapes." The duck leaves, but comes back to the bar the very next day and asks the bartender:" Got any grapes?" The bartender looks at the duck and says in kind of an irritated tone, "NO, we have no grapes here." So, the duck turns around and leaves, but comes in the bar the very next day and asks the bartender: "Got any grapes?" This makes the bartender extremely angry and he yells at the duck saying:" First of all Mr. Duck, NO we have NO grapes here! And secondly, if you come here tomorrow, I will nail your webbed feet to the friggin' floor!" So the duck leaves, but comes back the very next day and says to the bartender: "Got any nails?" The bartender tries to keep his composure and replies angrily to the duck: "NO we have no nails" So the duck then says:" Good, got any grapes?"

If Your Nose Runs, And Your Feet Smell, Are You Upside Down?

They say if 2 is company and 3 is a crowd, what is 4 and 5? Nine.

What's the leading cause of dry skin? Towels.

The banker saw his old friend Tom, an eighty-year-old rancher, in town. Tom lost his wife a year before and rumor had it that he was marrying a "mail order" bride. Being a good friend, the banker asked Tom if the rumor was true. Tom assured him that it was. The banker then asked Tom the age of his new bride to be. Tom proudly said, "She'll be twenty-one in November." Now the banker, being the wise man that he was, was worried that the sexual appetite of a young woman could not be satisfied by an eighty-year-old man. Wanting his friend's remaining

If Your Nose Runs, And Your Feet Smell, Are You Upside Down?

years to be happy, the banker tactfully suggested that Tom should consider getting a hired hand to help him out on the ranch, knowing nature would take its own course. Tom thought this was a good idea and said he would look for one that afternoon. About four months later, the banker ran into Tom in town again. "How's the new wife?" asked the banker. Tom proudly said, "Oh, she's pregnant." The banker, happy that his sage advice had worked out, continued, "And how's the hired hand?" Without hesitating, Tom said, "She's pregnant too."

A young girl was talking to her aunt about her protesting days way back in the 60's. "Aunty, were there a lot of protests?" The aunt replied that there were plenty of them. "Aunty, did a lot of people get into trouble

If Your Nose Runs, And Your Feet Smell, Are You Upside Down?

during the protests?" The aunt replied "It was a different time back in those days and we were protesting about war and peace. The police officers or as we called them 'the fuzz' used to arrest a lot of protesters." The girl thought about it and asked "Aunty? Did you ever get picked up by the fuzz?" The aunt thought a second and then replied "No, but I've been swung around by the tits a couple of times."

When I get naked in the bathroom, the shower gets turned on.

Yesterday, I fell off a 30 ft ladder. Thank God, I was only on the third step.
Brains are wonderful, I wish everyone had one.

If Your Nose Runs, And Your Feet Smell, Are You Upside Down?

Don't condemn nudists - they were born like this.

Moses has been guiding his people through the desert for 40 years. So, I guess even way back then, we males didn't stop to ask for directions.

It's very difficult to be dumb these days. The competition is simply too big.

I know my drinking limits. The problem is that I can never reach them – I simply fall down.

Alcohol! Because no great story started with someone eating a salad.

If Your Nose Runs, And Your Feet Smell, Are You Upside Down?

My wallet is like an onion. When I open it, it makes me cry...

Alcohol doesn't solve any problems, but neither does milk.

Nowadays you need a fixed telephone line only to find your smartphone.

WHY whenever I sit down to work, someone wakes me up?

ETC.----End of Thinking Capacity.

I drink water sometimes on the weekends to surprise my liver.

If Your Nose Runs, And Your Feet Smell, Are You Upside Down?

Al Gore said he invented the internet. Oh? I suppose he will say he invented the ALGORITHM as well?

You know it's cold outside, when you go outside............ and its cold

What smells like bananas, tastes like bananas, feels like bananas, but isn't bananas? Monkey poop.

If Your Nose Runs, And Your Feet Smell, Are
You Upside Down?

BLONDE

A blonde was talking to her friend about past
lovers. The friend told the blonde, "I slept
with a Brazilian." The blonde looked at her
friend in great confusion and said, "Gee, how
many is a Brazilian?"

More than 75% of people will try to lick their
elbow, after reading this fact for the first
time.

What did the blonde say when she looked
into a box of Cheerios? "Oh look! Donut
seeds!"

If Your Nose Runs, And Your Feet Smell, Are You Upside Down?

What do you call a really smart blonde? A golden retriever.

Two blondes fell down a hole. One said, 'It's dark in here isn't it?' The other replied, 'I don't know; I can't see.'

Why did the blonde stare at frozen orange juice can for 2 hours? Because it said 'concentrate'.

Why can't a blonde dial 911? She can't find the eleven on the phone.

If Your Nose Runs, And Your Feet Smell, Are You Upside Down?

How come it takes so long to build a blonde snowman? Because you have to hollow out the head.

Did you hear about the new blonde paint? It's not real bright, but it's cheap, and spreads easy.

Why do blondes wear underwear? To keep their ankles warm.

How can you get a blonde to laugh on Saturday? Tell her a joke on Wednesday.

Why don't blondes get coffee breaks? It takes too long to retrain them.

If Your Nose Runs, And Your Feet Smell, Are You Upside Down?

Why was the blonde confused after giving birth to twins? She couldn't figure out who the other mother was.

A blonde, brunette, and redhead are in the ninth grade; which one is the sexiest? The blonde, because she is the only one that's 18.

Why do blondes wash their hair in the sink? Because that's where your supposed to wash vegetables.

Two blondes are on opposite sides of a wide and deep stream. One blonde yells to the other, "How do I get on the other side?" The other blonde yell back to her, "You ARE on the other side."

If Your Nose Runs, And Your Feet Smell, Are You Upside Down?

A Television game show host asked a very ditzy blonde contestant the following question: "Contestant number one, for $500.00, if you were in a vacuum, and someone yelled FIRE!!!! Could you hear it?" The blonde looks at him and thinks about it for a second and says, "Is the vacuum on or off?"

A Brunette comes home and tells her blonde roommate that there is a rumor going around that Professor Brown from down the hall was gay. Surprised, the blonde said "Wow, I have been sleeping with him for 6 months and didn't know he was a professor?"

If Your Nose Runs, And Your Feet Smell, Are
You Upside Down?

A blonde and a brunette were speeding down
an old country road when a state trooper
started in pursuit of them. The blonde said,
"Don't look now, but a police car is chasing
us." The brunette said to the blonde, "Are
his lights on?" The blonde replied, "Yes, no,
yes, no, yes, no.......".

Brunette: "Where were you born?"
Blonde: "California."
Brunette: "Which part?"
Blonde: "All of me."

If Your Nose Runs, And Your Feet Smell, Are
You Upside Down?

OTHER STUFF

What did the bra say to the hat? "You go on
a head, I'll stay here and give these 2 a lift."

I haven't slept for three days, because I
think that would be way too long.

A computer once beat me at chess, but it
was no match for me at kick boxing.

This happens to everyone – when you don't
know how to spell a word, you think of a
whole new sentence to avoid using it.

If Your Nose Runs, And Your Feet Smell, Are
You Upside Down?

The IQ test showed that she is extremely
beautiful.

If you had a 12" penis growing out of your
forehead, would you be able to see the tip? I
doubt it, the balls would be hanging in your
eyes.

What's the best thing about Switzerland? I
don't know, but the flag is a big plus.

Can a kangaroo jump higher than the Empire
State Building? Of course. The Empire State
Building can't jump.

If Your Nose Runs, And Your Feet Smell, Are
You Upside Down?

Doctor: You're overweight.
Patient: I think I want a second opinion.
Doctor: You're also ugly.

If 4 out of 5 people SUFFER from diarrhea;
does that mean that one of those 5 enjoy it?

Whoever said technology would replace all
paper obviously hasn't tried wiping their ass
with an iPad.

I won $3 million on the lottery this weekend
so I decided to donate a quarter of it to
charity. Now I have $2,999,999.75.

If Your Nose Runs, And Your Feet Smell, Are You Upside Down?

I was at an ATM and this old lady asked me to help check her balance, so I pushed her over.

People say I'm condescending. That means that I talk down to people.

Which country's capital is the fastest growing? Ireland's. Every year it's Dublin.

A Spanish magician has a huge and elaborate magic show and at the end he says he will disappear after counting to three. He starts to count, "Un, dos..." Bammm! He vanished without a tres.

If Your Nose Runs, And Your Feet Smell, Are You Upside Down?

What's the difference between a cat and a complex sentence? A cat has claws at the end of its paws. A complex sentence has a pause at the end of its clause.

What's the difference between roast beef and pea soup? Anyone can roast beef, but nobody can pea soup!

Why can't you trust what an atom says? Because they make up literally everything.

A 7-year-old and a 4-year-old are in their bedroom. "You know what?" says the 7-year-old, "I think it's time we started swearing. When we go downstairs for breakfast, I'll swear first, then you." "Okay," replies the 4-

If Your Nose Runs, And Your Feet Smell, Are You Upside Down?

year-old. In the kitchen, when the mother asks the 7-year-old what he wants for breakfast, he answers, "I'll have oatmeal bitch." She slaps him across the face so hard he flies off the chair, crying his eyes out. The mother looks at the 4-year-old & sternly asks, "And what would YOU like? The kid looks at her in fear and says "I don't know, but it won't be the oatmeal.

A guy is going on an ocean cruise and he tells his doctor that he's worried about getting seasick. The doctor suggests, "Eat two pounds of stewed tomatoes before you leave the dock." The guy replies, "Will that keep me from getting sick, Doc?" The doctor says, "No, but it'll look really pretty in the water."

If Your Nose Runs, And Your Feet Smell, Are
You Upside Down?

What do you call a cow with no
legs? Hamburger.

How can you drop a raw egg onto a concrete
floor without cracking it?
You can't crack a concrete floor with an egg.

If tomatoes are fruit, shouldn't ketchup be
considered a smoothie?

Why do the French eat snails? They don't like
fast food.

What's red and bad for your teeth? A brick.

If Your Nose Runs, And Your Feet Smell, Are You Upside Down?

Here is an ego booster for you:
Step 1: Name your iPhone "Titanic."
Step 2: Plug it into your computer.
Step 3: When iTunes says, "Titanic is syncing," press cancel.
Step 4: Now you can say you saved the Titanic. Feel like a hero?

Have you heard about the new restaurant called Karma? There's no menu; you get what you deserve.

Gandhi often walked barefoot, which produced an impressive set of callouses on his feet. He also ate very little, making him rather frail and with his odd diet, he often suffered from bad breath. This made him a super calloused fragile mystic hexed with halitosis.

If Your Nose Runs, And Your Feet Smell, Are You Upside Down?

Why can't orphans play baseball? Because they don't know where home is.

How do you make holy water? Boil the hell out of it.

Innkeeper: "The room is $95 a night, but it's only $5 if you make your own bed."
Guest: "I'll make my own bed."
Innkeeper: "Good. I'll get you some nails and wood."

What do cats eat for breakfast? Mice Krispies.

If Your Nose Runs, And Your Feet Smell, Are
You Upside Down?

What did the green grape say to the purple
grape? "Breathe, stupid!"

Whenever I fart out loud in a public, I just
yell, "Turbo power!" and walk faster.

Teacher: "If I gave you 2 cats and another 2
cats and another 2, how many would you
have?"
Billy: "Seven."
Teacher: "No, listen carefully... If I gave you
two cats, and another two cats and another
two, how many would you have?"
Billy: "Seven."
Teacher: "Let me put it to you differently. If I
gave you two apples, and another two apples
and another two, how many would you
have?"

If Your Nose Runs, And Your Feet Smell, Are You Upside Down?

Billy: "Six."
Teacher: "Good. Now if I gave you two cats, and another two cats and another two, how many would you have?"
Billy: "Seven!"
Teacher: "Now Billy, where the heck do you get seven from?!"
Billy: "Because I've already got a friggin' cat!"

Teacher: "Kids, what does the chicken give you?"
Student: "Meat!"
Teacher: "Very good! Now what does the pig give you?"
Student: "Bacon!"
Teacher: "Great! And what does the fat cow give you?"
Student: "Homework!"

If Your Nose Runs, And Your Feet Smell, Are You Upside Down?

A teacher instructs his students to stand up and use the word 'Definitely' in a sentence. Phillip raises his hand and says, "I definitely want to be a professional wrestler when I grow up".

"Very good Phillip," the teacher said. "Anyone else?" Ruth raised her hand and said, "I definitely can't wait for the weekend." Very good. Anyone else?" Dirty Tommy raised his hand and said, "Teacher, I have a question before I make a sentence."

The teacher asks Dirty Tommy what the question was. "Are farts lumpy?" The whole class started to laugh hysterically. The teacher tells the class to quiet down and tells Dirty Tommy they don't use that type of language in the classroom. So, Dirty Tommy asked him again, "Teacher, I really need to know. Are farts lumpy?" and the classy starts laughing hysterically again. So, just to move

If Your Nose Runs, And Your Feet Smell, Are You Upside Down?

on the teacher says "I will answer the question, but then you have to make the sentence. No, Farts are NOT lumpy." Dirty Tommy looks at the teacher and says, "Well then, my sentence is: "Farts are not lumpy, therefore, I definitely shit my pants."

I heard a great joke about amnesia, but I forgot it.

If Your Nose Runs, And Your Feet Smell, Are You Upside Down?

Men and Women

Scientists have discovered a food that diminishes a woman's sex drive by 90%. It's called a wedding cake.

I haven't spoken to my wife in three weeks. I didn't want to interrupt her.

I think I have found a new meaning for PMS. I think it means Punish My Spouse.

Morning sex is the best thing to wake up to…. That is, unless you are in prison.

If Your Nose Runs, And Your Feet Smell, Are You Upside Down?

A recent survey says that the average woman would better choose to be beautiful than to have brains. I guess that's because the average man can see better than he thinks.

What did the cannibal do after dumping his girlfriend?
He wiped his ass.

Women spend their whole lives to find the right man, just to tell him every day, that he is wrong.

Is Google male or female?
Female, because it doesn't let you finish a sentence before making a suggestion.

If Your Nose Runs, And Your Feet Smell, Are You Upside Down?

One day, a man came home and was greeted by his wife dressed in stunningly sexy lingerie. "Tie me up," she purred, "And you can do anything you want." So, he tied her up and went golfing.

A wife says to her husband, "Our new neighbor always kisses his wife when he leaves for work. Why don't you do that?" The husband replied, "How can I? I don't even know her."

I have a buddy who is about three years into his relationship now and he started to have erection problems. So, he and his woman had different ideas as to what the problem is: She bought him some Viagra and he bought her a treadmill.

If Your Nose Runs, And Your Feet Smell, Are You Upside Down?

If you want to know who a man's best friend is really, put your dog and your wife in the trunk of your car, come back an hour later, open the trunk, and see which one is happy to see you.

My friend asked me, "Why are you getting a divorce?" I responded, "My wife wasn't home the entire night and, in the morning,, she said she spent the night at her sister's house." He said, "So?" And I responded, "She's lying. I spent the night at her sister's house!"

A man asks his wife, "What would you do if I won the lottery?" His wife says, "Take half and leave your sorry ass!" The man replies, "Oh Hallelujah! I won 12 bucks, here is six, now get the hell out!"

If Your Nose Runs, And Your Feet Smell, Are
You Upside Down?

A woman was taking an afternoon nap. When
she woke up, she told her husband, "I just
dreamed that you gave me a pearl necklace.
What do you think it means?" "You'll know
tonight," he said. That evening, the man
came home with a small package and gave it
to his wife. Delighted, she opened it to find a
book entitled, "The Meaning of Dreams."

A wife asked her husband, "Honey, will you
still love me when I am old and overweight?"
The man replied, "Yes, I do."

I married Miss Right. I just didn't know her
first name was Always.

I think I married a nun.......nun tonight, nun
tomorrow...........

If Your Nose Runs, And Your Feet Smell, Are You Upside Down?

Only newlyweds and liars have sex every day.

A man admitted he lied on his income tax return: he listed himself as the head of the household!

Marriage is the main reason for divorce.

How do you paralyze a woman from the waist down? Marry her.

The wife said to the husband, you're fat! The husband said, I'm not fat, ... I'm just easier to see.

If Your Nose Runs, And Your Feet Smell, Are You Upside Down?

If you prepare for the divorce, the wedding is much nicer.

If Your Nose Runs, And Your Feet Smell, Are You Upside Down?

FAMOUS STUFF

What's the difference between Whitney Houston and Whitney Houston jokes? The jokes will get old.

Why did Whitney Houston snort artificial sweetener? She thought it was diet coke.

What kind of car Do Jedi's drive? A ToYODA.

What do you call a bounty hunter from the South? Bubba Fett.

If Your Nose Runs, And Your Feet Smell, Are
You Upside Down?

What do you call someone who doesn't like
the dark side? A: Darth Hater.

What side of an Ewok has the most hair? The
outside.

What do you call a Sith with a lisp who won't
fight? A Sithy.

What do you call a potato that has turned to
the Dark side? Vader Tots.

Why did the angry Jedi cross the road? To
get to the Dark Side.

If Your Nose Runs, And Your Feet Smell, Are
You Upside Down?

What does Michael Jackson and a Nintendo
have in common? They are both made of
plastic and kids turn them on.

Did you see Dolly Parton's new shoes?
Neither did she.

Why are Dolly Parton's feet so small?
Nothing grows in the shade.

What does Woody Allen call an unborn baby?
A blind date.

What does JFK Jr. miss most about Martha's
Vineyard? The runway.

If Your Nose Runs, And Your Feet Smell, Are
You Upside Down?

What was JFK Jr. drinking at the time of the
crash? Ocean Spray.

What is forty feet long and has eight teeth
and the IQ of 12? The front row at a country
music concert.

How do Helen Keller's parents punish her? By
putting a plunger in the toilet.

What is the name of Helen Keller's dog? A.
Nyah, nyu, yuh, yah

Why did Helen Keller's dog committed
suicide? If your name was Nyah, nyu, yuh,
yah, you'd commit suicide too.

If Your Nose Runs, And Your Feet Smell, Are You Upside Down?

What's the name of the new game that Bill and Monica were playing in the White House? Swallow the Leader.

What does Dale Earnhardt and Pink Floyd have in common? Their last great hit was the wall.

What does Eric Clapton and a cup of coffee have in common? They both suck without Cream.

What would Will Smith leave behind if he ever committed a crime? Fresh Prints.

If Your Nose Runs, And Your Feet Smell, Are You Upside Down?

How did Helen Keller's mother punish her? By rearranging the living-room furniture.

What did Helen Keller do when she fell down the well? She screamed her fingers off.

Why does Helen Keller masturbate with one hand? So, she can moan with the other.

Why was Helen Keller's leg yellow? Her dog was blind too.

What did Helen Keller's parents do to punish her for swearing? Washed her hands with soap.

If Your Nose Runs, And Your Feet Smell, Are
You Upside Down?

How come Mike Tyson's eye's water during
sex? Mace.

Why shouldn't Democrats worry about losing
the midterm elections? Apparently,
depression is covered by Obamacare.

What does Barack Obama call illegal aliens?
Undocumented democrats.

Why did Anna Nicole Smith change her hair
color from blonde to red? Because red is
easier to spell!

If Your Nose Runs, And Your Feet Smell, Are You Upside Down?

What does Jack Nicholson's portrayal of the Joker have that Heath Ledger's doesn't? A chance for a sequel.

What's the difference between me and Heath Ledger? Heath's Better looking, but I woke up this morning.

Harrison Ford is getting so old, his next movie is going to be called "Indiana Bones and The Battle with Osteoporosis."

I won't watch a Nicolas Cage movie, unless it's done in 60 seconds.

If Your Nose Runs, And Your Feet Smell, Are You Upside Down?

Why did Bruce Willis pop a couple of Viagra's before fighting terrorists? He thought it was "A Good Day to Die Hard".

What did Mark Wahlberg feed Ted? Nothing, he was already stuffed.

Why can't you give Elsa a balloon? Because she will Let it go.

If Your Nose Runs, And Your Feet Smell, Are
You Upside Down?

CONFUCIUS SAY.....

CONFUCIUS SAY..... Life isn't like a box of chocolates. It's more like a jar of jalapenos. What you do today, might burn your butt tomorrow.

CONFUCIUS SAY..... If the world didn't suck, we all would fall off.

CONFUCIUS SAY..... Inside every older person is a younger person wondering, 'What the hell happened?'

CONFUCIUS SAY..... Light travels faster than sound. That's why some people appear bright until you hear them speak.

If Your Nose Runs, And Your Feet Smell, Are
You Upside Down?

CONFUCIUS SAY..... When everything is
coming your way, you're in the wrong lane.

CONFUCIUS SAY..... Change is inevitable,
except from vending machines.

CONFUCIUS SAY.....A clear conscience is
usually the sign of a bad memory.

CONFUCIUS SAY..... Eagles may soar, but
weasels don't get sucked into jet engines.

CONFUCIUS SAY..... Hard work pays off in
the future. Laziness pays off now.

If Your Nose Runs, And Your Feet Smell, Are You Upside Down?

CONFUCIUS SAY..... Depression is merely anger without enthusiasm.

CONFUCIUS SAY..... What happens if you get scared half to death, twice?

CONFUCIUS SAY..... There are two kinds of pedestrians: the quick and the dead.

CONFUCIUS SAY..... Health is merely the slowest possible rate at which one can die.

CONFUCIUS SAY..... The only difference between a rut and a grave is the depth.

If Your Nose Runs, And Your Feet Smell, Are
You Upside Down?

CONFUCIUS SAY..... The early bird may get
the worm, but the second mouse gets the
cheese.

CONFUCIUS SAY..... He who laughs last,
thinks slowest.

CONFUCIUS SAY..... Half the people you
know are below average.

CONFUCIUS SAY..... Acupuncture is a jab
well done.

CONFUCIUS SAY.....5 out of 4 people are
bad in math.

If Your Nose Runs, And Your Feet Smell, Are
You Upside Down?

CONFUCIUS SAY.....A will is a dead
giveaway.

CONFUCIUS SAY.....A day without sunshine
is like night.

CONFUCIUS SAY.....62.7 percent of all
statistics are made up on the spot.

CONFUCIUS SAY.....99 percent of Politicians
give the rest a bad name.

CONFUCIUS SAY..... Life is sexually
transmitted.

If Your Nose Runs, And Your Feet Smell, Are
You Upside Down?

CONFUCIUS SAY..... To write with a broken
pencil is pointless.

CONFUCIUS SAY.....A bicycle can't stand
alone; it is two tired.

CONFUCIUS SAY..... No matter how much
you push the envelope, it will always be
stationery.

CONFUCIUS SAY..... A boiled egg is hard to
beat.

CONFUCIUS SAY..... Those who get too big
for their britches will be exposed in the end.

I hope you enjoyed this first book…..
CAUTION, OTHERS MAY FOLLOW!!!!!!

A special thank you to the following that helped mold me, some good, annnnnd some not so good:
Jesus, The Almighty God, Dad, The Town of DERBY, CONNECTICUT, Catherine, Philly Cheese Steak, Bug, Harold Petz (Grampa), Carolyn Petz,(Grammie) , Ed "Fast Eddie" Petz, J. Jerry 'the artist' Petz, Carrie Sharkey, Scott S.D., Dr. Donald A. Davis, Margaret Davis, Rod and Beth Kukait, Carmen Perri, Zeny, Tessie, Beth S.D., Jeff W.D., And Dad T.D., Susan J.D., Betty D. Bob Shortell, Ann and Pete Massa, Alex Inawat, D.U.M.C, Sally Roberts, Charlie Clark, Emmett O'Brien Regional Vocational Technical School, Shirley Sabo, Richard Marazzi, George Sender, Jack Marchitto, Harris Plaisted, Frank DiManno, Freddie M., B.H. May, The Peyton Families, The Inawat family, Bob & Dee Hoyt, Jessica Duran, Ross Sessions, Dale O, Tee W, Maricela R, Amparo E, Cheryl Z. Mark W. The City of PALMDALE, CA, The Dr's, nurses and staff at Henry Mayo Newhall Hospital that kept me alive when I should have been dead a long time ago, Ryan Kerrigan, And a shout out to my team that makes me laugh and sob hysterically every season- HTTR!!!!

I intend to live forever. *__So far, So good.__*
\- Don Davis

Book 2- Coming Soon!